Oliver Twist

Written by Charles Dickens
Adapted by Benjamin Hulme-Cross
Illustrated by Andy Elkerton

Published by Pearson Education Limited,
80 Strand, London, WC2R 0RL.

www.pearsonschools.co.uk

Text © Pearson Education Limited 2017

Designed by Karen Awadzi Red Giraffe
Original illustrations © Pearson Education Limited 2017
Illustrated by Andy Elkerton

First published 2017

21 20 19 18 17
10 9 8 7 6 5 4 3 2 1

British Library Cataloguing in Publication Data
A catalogue record for this book is available
from the British Library

ISBN 978 0 435 18630 2

Printed in the UK by Ashford Colour Press

CONTENTS

CHAPTER 1

A DIFFICULT BEGINNING

OLIVER TWIST was born into a cruel world.

The weary surgeon who attended his birth had delivered too many babies born of unmarried mothers who had nowhere else to turn but the workhouse. Yet his heart still stirred at the sight of the beautiful young woman who lay before him, begging to hold her baby.

"Please!" the young woman whispered. "Just once before I die."

A careworn old nurse shook her head and tutted. "She shouldn't talk of dying now, bless 'er! When she's 'ad thirteen babies like me, and all but two of 'em dead, and them other two living in the workhouse with me, then she might talk of dying!"

The surgeon knew that the young woman did not have long to live though, and he placed baby Oliver in her arms. She looked down at the feeble infant and brushed her lips against his forehead. It was to be her final act in this world.

There was precious little that was good about growing up in a workhouse. The poor and unfortunate were expected to work almost constantly, as if being poor and unfortunate were something that deserved punishment.

As the years passed, Oliver learned to accept his fate – he had never known anything different. Like the other orphans in the workhouse, Oliver found very little time (and even less energy) to play. The only thing that brought Oliver any comfort was dreaming about a different life, one with a family, but he kept that thought to himself.

The workhouse was run by a miserable creature named Mrs Mann, a woman so selfish that she stole most of the money she was supposed to use to buy food for the boys. Consequently, the food rations were awfully light. In fact, all that Oliver and the other orphans ever ate was a sort of thin, watery porridge called gruel.

Oliver was ten years old by the time a new boy joined the workhouse. A butcher's son whose father had got into debt, the new boy was used to eating meat at every meal and it did not take too many bowls of gruel before he became extremely agitated.

"Why can't we ask for some meat?" the butcher's son wanted to know. "Or at least some seconds!" A couple of the others smirked. They knew they would likely be beaten if they were so rude.

The room in which the boys were fed was a large stone hall with a copper pot at one end out of which the master ladled the gruel at mealtimes. Each boy had one bowlful of gruel and not a drop more, except at Christmas when they were also given a slice of bread.

The bowls never needed washing. The hungry boys scraped them with their spoons till they shone again, and when they had finished they would sit staring at the copper pot, sucking their fingers in case any gruel had splashed their hands.

The butcher's boy could take no more, he said, and if he didn't get a proper meal soon he feared he might have to eat the boy who slept in the bunk next to his. Thin and starving, Oliver and the others were slowly coming round to the idea of asking the master for more, and they decided to draw lots.

It was Oliver Twist who drew the short straw, and this chance event was to change his life forever.

The evening arrived and the boys took their places in the dining hall. The master, in his cook's uniform, stood by the pot and the gruel was served out. As usual, it disappeared from the bowls in seconds, and the boys began whispering to each other and nudging Oliver.

Miserable, hungry and desperate, he stood, walked the length of the long hall with spoon and bowl in hand, and stopped in front of the master.

"Please, sir," he said in a small voice. "I want some more."

The master turned very pale and stared at Oliver for a few moments, wondering how any of the boys could have the cheek to ask for more food.

"What?" the master eventually croaked, in a faint voice.

"Please, sir," replied Oliver, "I want some more."

The master had by now recovered his composure and did what any reasonable man would do in his position. He called for assistance, grabbed Oliver by the arm and aimed a blow at the boy's head with the ladle.

So that was why, some days later, Oliver found himself sold on by the workhouse, who wanted rid of this troublesome boy before he stirred a rebellious spirit in the other orphans.

He was to become an undertaker's apprentice, and though he was not sorry to be leaving the workhouse, Oliver was a bag of nerves on the night he was delivered to his new master.

Mr Sowerberry, the undertaker, seemed pleasant enough. His wife, however, was as unfriendly as most of the adults Oliver had encountered in his life at the workhouse.

"He's a bit small!" said Mrs Sowerberry, when she saw Oliver. "Probably cost us more in food than he'll bring in by working, I dare say! These children always cost more to keep than they're worth."

"Nonsense, my dear!" said the undertaker, cheerfully. "Take him down to the basement and get him something to eat. He can have those scraps of meat we were saving for the dog."

Meat! Oliver's eyes grew round and his mouth began watering uncontrollably.

By the time he went to sleep among the coffins in the undertaker's shop, Oliver was beginning to think that his luck might be turning.

Sadly, though, the life of an undertaker was not to be Oliver's. Mr Sowerberry had another apprentice, a much older lad named Noah, who took an instant dislike to Oliver and spent the next few weeks trying to goad the young newcomer into some act of violence, in the hope that he might be sent back to the workhouse.

Oliver did his best to ignore the provocation, until the older boy finally hit upon the subject of Oliver's mother, and began teasing him mercilessly.

"Workhouse," said Noah, for that is what he called Oliver, "how's your mother?"

"She's dead," replied Oliver, his cheeks darkening. "Don't you say anything about her to me!"

"What did she die of, Workhouse?" said Noah.

"Of a broken heart, some of our old nurses told me," replied Oliver, more as if he were talking to himself than answering Noah.

"You know, Workhouse," continued Noah, "from what I heard your mother was a right bad one! Better that she's dead, that's what I heard."

Crimson with fury, Oliver leapt up and punched Noah as hard as he could. The older boy dropped to the ground and began wailing.

"He'll murder me!" blubbered Noah. "Mr Sowerberry! Help, sir, help! Oliver's gone mad, sir!"

When the undertaker appeared, Oliver was still too angry to speak, leaving Noah to paint a picture of an unprovoked attack. Shaking with silent fury, Oliver was locked in the basement where the coffins were kept.

That night, Oliver overheard talk of his being returned to the workhouse. He simply could not face that prospect, and it made up his mind. He would run away to London and seek his fortune in a place where he might at least be his own master.

He climbed up on the coffins, opened a window, and crept out into the night.

CHAPTER 2

LONDON AND NEW FRIENDS

AFTER a few days' trudge, a few nights spent sleeping in hedges, and shoes worn down by the long, hard walk, Oliver arrived in London. He sat down on the kerb, gawping at the new sights and sounds and smells of the city, dazed and exhausted.

"'Ello there, friend, what's your game?" Oliver started, his reverie broken, and looked up to see a boy about his own age staring down at him. He was the most peculiar looking person Oliver had ever seen. The boy did not seem wealthy – quite the opposite – but he had the confidence of a wealthy gentleman. He wore a man's coat down to his heels, a large hat that wobbled loosely on top of his head, and corduroy trousers into whose pockets his hands were thrust.

Oliver was so exhausted, and so grateful to see a friendly face that he found the words tumbling out. He explained that he was alone, that he'd been walking for days with barely any food, that he needed somewhere to sleep. All the while the stranger listened intently, nodding thoughtfully from time to time until Oliver had finished.

"What's your name then, friend?" The boy asked, and when Oliver had introduced himself the boy stuck out his hand. "I'm Dodger," he said. "'The Artful Dodger' as some call me. Your luck's in, old son. It so 'appens a friend of mine 'as a spare bed and 'e likes nothing better than looking out for children what need 'elp. You interested? Then follow me!"

Dodger strolled through London as if he owned the city: chest puffed out, hands in pockets and a big grin on his face. He bought them both a hearty meal and led the way to a rougher part of the city. Oliver was suddenly acutely aware that he was in a bad place. There were filthy children everywhere and the only places showing any sign of prosperity were the taverns, in which shady characters argued and fought loudly. He was on the point of running away, when Dodger took him by the arm and pushed him through the door of a house that opened directly onto the street.

"Now then! It's Dodger and a new pal!" Dodger called out, leading Oliver up a narrow, creaking stairway and through another doorway. The walls and ceiling of the room they entered were black with age and dirt. There was a frying pan on the fire, in which sausages were cooking, and next to the fire stood a laundry rail, completely covered with silk handkerchiefs of all colours and watched over by a hunched, red-bearded old man. A group of boys were sitting around a table, and Dodger made his way over to them, as did the old man.

There was a whispered conversation, then all of them turned to face Oliver and grinned.

"This is 'im, Fagin," said Dodger; "my friend, Oliver Twist."

"How pleased I am to make your acquaintance, sir," said Fagin, bowing low to the ground. "We never say no to an extra set of fingers, eh boys?" This set the others sniggering, although Oliver did not understand the joke.

In any case, the old man and the boys were friendly enough, and the sausages were good, and while the dirty room was not anyone's idea of a perfect home, there was a bed in it for Oliver. He slumped onto it after dinner with an exhausted sigh, and fell instantly asleep.

In the middle of the night Oliver woke, though he could have been dreaming – he was not certain. In a shaft of moonlight he saw Fagin on the floor, hunched over a small wooden chest and counting out various treasures: fine jewellery, gold pocket watches and fancy silk handkerchiefs.

The next morning, he woke to find the room empty save for Fagin. "Now, young Master Oliver," said Fagin, after a hearty breakfast had been consumed. "As the others have all gone out to work, perhaps I may spend the day educating you so that tomorrow you can go to work as well."

"I'd like that very much, Mr Fagin, thank you," replied Oliver.

"Fagin you old goat!" came a female voice from the doorway. "This one talks like a right young gentleman. Where did you find 'im then?"

"He's come to make his fortune in London," said Fagin, sounding annoyed. "And kindly don't creep up on me like a thief, Nancy, or you may get hurt."

Oliver stared at Nancy. She was in her twenties, she was pretty, and she had the kindest face Oliver could remember having seen in a long while.

"Does the fine young gentleman 'ave a name then?" she said, looking at Oliver and smiling. Oliver swallowed and gave a little bow.

"Oliver Twist, miss. It's a pleasure to make your acquaintance."

"Oh bless 'im, 'e really is like a young gentleman. Fagin, even you should know better: 'e don't belong in a place like this."

"Mind your business, and I'll mind mine," Fagin grumbled.

"Actually it's business I'm 'ere about," said Nancy, briskly. "Bill says you're late with your payment and I'm to collect it."

"Bill Sikes is a thief!" Fagin hissed, but he handed over some money all the same.

"Much obliged, Fagin, much obliged," said Nancy, turning to go. "It was lovely to meet you Oliver."

The next morning, Fagin told Oliver to accompany Dodger and a boy called Charley

Bates to learn about the work they did. Once again Dodger ambled through the streets as if he owned them. He was happy to answer Oliver's questions, except those about work.

"You'll see soon enough," he kept saying. On the topics of Nancy and Bill, though, he was more forthcoming. Oliver learned that Bill was Nancy's sweetheart, and that everyone in the city was afraid of him.

"Hey, Dodger!" Charley cut in. "Over there! He'll do!" He pointed across the street to a respectable-looking old man who was standing outside a shop, reading a book. He seemed completely lost in the pages.

"Wait 'ere," Dodger hissed, and he and Charley made their way across the street. To Oliver's astonishment, he watched Dodger reach into the gentleman's pocket and pull out a silk handkerchief, before darting away around a corner with Charley. The gentleman frowned, reached into his pocket and looked up.

In a panic, Oliver turned and ran down the street. The gentleman saw a young boy tearing

away and shouted "Stop! Thief!" at the top of his lungs.

It will come as no surprise to learn that young Oliver was soon caught. A swift visit to the courthouse followed, and it was only the last minute evidence of a shopkeeper who had seen what really happened that kept Oliver out of real trouble.

The gentleman whose handkerchief had been stolen was horrified at the thought of the injustice that had nearly occurred.

"Allow me to apologise properly," said the gentleman, taking Oliver by the arm and escorting him down the steps of the courthouse. "I am Mr Brownlow, at your service. I do hope that you can forgive me for wrongly accusing you?"

Oliver nodded, too overwhelmed by everything that had happened to speak.

"You are most gracious," said Mr Brownlow.

"Now it seems clear to me that you are in need of a proper home. I wonder, would you do me the very great honour of coming to stay with me?"

Again, Oliver just nodded, and with that his circumstances changed once more.

Mr Brownlow helped Oliver into a carriage, and they made their way from the courthouse to a very pleasant and wealthy part of the city.

CHAPTER 3
TRUE FRIENDS AND TRUE ENEMIES

"I WON'T do it, Fagin!" said Nancy. "It ain't right. Oliver's just a boy, and not like the others, just a sweet little boy. Never did us any 'arm either!"

"Fagin, she'll do it alright, I'll make sure of that." Bill Sikes was with Nancy in Fagin's room, and his tone was menacing. Dodger and the other boys pressed themselves back against the walls of the room, praying that Bill didn't lose his temper. He was a thick set, dark haired, mean looking man without a trace of human kindness in him. Why Nancy should be in love with him was a mystery to all.

"Nancy, my dear," said Fagin. "Oliver knows

who we are and where we are and I don't need to tell you that none of us would fare too well before a judge now, do I?"

"That don't mean we should kidnap 'im!" Nancy protested.

"Who said anything about kidnapping?" Fagin replied in a soothing tone, rubbing his hands together. "We just need to bring him here so we can talk to him, that's all. And you're the only one he'll trust, my dear. It's been a week now since he went off with that Brownlow gentleman. He's bound to come out of the house sooner or later!"

"Like I said Fagin," growled Bill Sikes as Nancy burst into tears, "she'll do it."

Oliver had been resting at Mr Brownlow's house now for several days. A fever had overcome him on the evening after his arrest and trial, and Mr Brownlow's kindly housekeeper, Mrs Bedwin, had been nursing him back to full strength.

Mr Brownlow himself had kept out of the way, believing that Oliver needed uninterrupted rest, but soon enough the boy was up and about and asking where he was. So it was that one week after Oliver's arrival at Mr Brownlow's house, the two of them sat together for the first time in the old gentleman's study.

Oliver soon found that he trusted Mr Brownlow completely – a feeling he had not experienced before – and he happily poured out the sorry details of his life story, choking on the words as he spoke of his mother. He finished his story and sat back in his chair, and as he did so his gaze fell on a portrait that hung above the fireplace.

Something in Oliver's heart stirred. The woman in the picture was just so beautiful, and her expression was so sad and so kind …

At the same moment Mr Brownlow made a very curious observation, looking from

Oliver's enthralled face to the portrait and back again. *Their features are all but identical!* thought Mr Brownlow.

Oliver felt the sudden need for some air.

"Might I go for a walk, sir?"

The old gentleman coughed and blinked.

"Yes, I suppose so. I have a package of books that needs delivering to an address nearby. You can take it if you like. It's only ten minutes away."

"I'd like that very much, sir, thank you!" Mr Brownlow explained where the books were to be delivered to, and Oliver made his way downstairs and out into the street. He walked slowly, still thinking about the woman in the portrait, and paying no real attention to where he was going.

"Why, Oliver!" said a familiar female voice. "I thought I'd never see you again! Come 'ome to your poor mother this minute!"

"Nancy!" Oliver exclaimed, confused by what she had said but happy to see her.

"Little brute put me through 'ell – he's been missing for a week!" Nancy said loudly as a few passers-by stopped and stared.
"We thought 'e'd run away for good!"

"Nancy … what …?" Oliver stammered. Then a rough hand scragged him by the neck as Bill Sikes joined Nancy.

"You're coming back 'ome with us, Oliver." Bill growled. "Like it or not!"

Oliver was shaking with terror by the time Bill Sikes shoved him through Fagin's door to the jeers and taunts of Dodger and Charley.

"Oh, master Oliver," Fagin mocked. "You should have said you were coming and I'd have cooked something special."

Oliver saw the trouble he was in, and with unusual presence of mind, he turned and bolted back out into the street, screaming for help. It was no use. Dodger and Charley caught him and dragged him back within a minute.

Fagin stepped towards Oliver with a large stick and raised it to strike the boy.

"Not while I draw breath, you old pig!" Nancy shouted. "Ain't it enough I've brought 'im back to you? You leave 'im alone or I'll go to the police myself and we can all 'ang together!"

"You watch yourself, girl," growled Bill, grabbing her by the throat. "You ever think of betraying Bill Sikes and I'll shut your mouth for good."

"And as for you, young master Oliver," Bill went on, his voice dripping with menace. "You try and run one more time and I'll shut your mouth for good. And 'ers!" he jabbed a finger in Nancy's direction.

"Now, Bill …" Fagin began.

"Oh, you and all Fagin!" Bill Sikes spat. "We've got the boy back but I'll be keeping 'im. I've a job tonight that needs a small 'elper, and I think that'll be Oliver."

"Bill, Bill! The boy's mine. What do you want with him, eh? Take Dodger, or Charley, or any of the others but not him, Bill."

Bill Sikes stared intently at Fagin. "This boy's coming with me, Fagin, and maybe next time we meet you can tell me just why 'e should be quite so important to you …"

With that, he grabbed Oliver by the neck again and dragged him out into the street once more.

It was a damp, foggy night and the chill had Oliver's teeth chattering as Bill Sikes hoisted him up and through a high narrow window before lowering him down by his coat onto the floor inside.

"Remember," whispered Sikes, still holding onto Oliver's coat. "All you 'ave to do is open the door for me. Get it wrong and I swear to you …" he left the threat hanging, handed Oliver a small lantern, and let go of the coat.

Oliver began to make his way across a dark room. He was trying to think of a way of escaping when he heard a shout. Sikes called him back to the window but it was too late. A gunshot rang out, Oliver felt a burning pain in his arm and then he crashed to the floor.

He heard more shouts, then a kind, female voice.

"Why, he's just a poor young boy …"

CHAPTER 4

BILL SIKES'S TERRIBLE CRIME

ONCE again, Oliver found himself being nursed back to health by kind strangers. Far from turning him over to the police, the ladies who lived in the house that he had broken into saw that he was as much a victim of criminals as they were.

Mrs Maylie and her niece Rose offered Oliver every comfort and protection, moving him a short way outside London to recover in the countryside. The peace he felt was unlike anything he had ever known, and he began to forget about his misadventures with Fagin and the gang.

However, while Oliver was ready to forget, others were not …

Back in London, Fagin was deep in conversation with a very secretive gentleman by the name of Monks.

"You'll get your reward when Oliver's been shipped to Australia," said Monks. "Not with him resting up in the country!"

"The fault isn't mine," wheedled Fagin. "Bill Sikes insisted on taking him on the job."

"I insist that you find Oliver Twist and see to it that he is ruined. I won't have blood on my hands, but get him convicted and sent away. Then you'll get your money."

"Mr Monks, you may be sure I will get rid of the boy. In the meanwhile you must pursue your own side of the plan and get rid of all evidence from the workhouse."

Monks gave a sudden start and rushed to the window. "Who's that?" he rasped, as a woman's shadow disappeared along the street.

"Calm yourself, young man," said Fagin. "We are safe here; I have eyes everywhere. I know where the boy is and when the time's right I'll find a way of acquiring him once again …"

You may have guessed that the shadow outside the window belonged to Nancy, whose conscience had overcome her fear of Bill Sikes and Fagin. Nor was that the first time she had spied on Fagin and Monks. In the course of her very dangerous investigations, she had discovered a great deal of information relating to Oliver Twist and the various dangers that he faced.

Armed with this information, she sent word the next day to the two people whom she knew had Oliver's true interests at heart, namely Mr Brownlow and the boy's new protector, Rose Maylie, instructing both of them to meet her on London Bridge.

Nancy was so worried for Oliver that she did not look around once as she made her way to the meeting. Had she looked back, she would have seen one of Fagin's gang following her, just within earshot.

As soon as she saw Mr Brownlow and Rose, the words came pouring out and Nancy told them everything she knew.

Mr Brownlow and Rose Maylie listened, aghast, as the extent of the plotting against Oliver became clear.

"So Fagin wants Oliver because this Monks character is paying him a reward?" Mr Brownlow's voice was strained.

"That's right Mr Brownlow, sir," said Nancy. "And Monks 'as been to Oliver's 'ometown and all. Been to the workhouse where he found something. And once he'd found it, he got rid of it."

By the time Nancy bade them farewell, Mr Brownlow and Rose understood very clearly just how much danger Oliver was in.

At length Rose said in a shaky voice, "What I don't understand is why Monks would care about getting rid of a boy who grew up in a workhouse. It just doesn't make sense!"

"I am beginning to think I may have the answer to all of this, Miss Maylie," said Mr Brownlow. "I hope you will forgive me if I make my own investigation before I share my suspicions with you. For now, you keep Oliver safe and I will do my best to track down Mr Monks …"

The atmosphere in Fagin's room crackled with tension. The boys were in a state of shock. Dodger had been caught pickpocketing and had been arrested, and Charley Bates had just recounted how the trial had progressed. Dodger had been sentenced to be shipped to Australia.

"No, no!" wailed Fagin. "Not Dodger! Not the best of my boys!"

"Serves 'im right for getting caught, the cocky fool!" said Bill Sikes. "I always said you should keep a better watch on what your little rats get up to."

"Oh, is that right, Mr Sikes," said Fagin, nastily. "Is that right? And what if I were to tell you that you should keep a better watch on what your little woman gets up to, eh?"

Bill made a lunge for Fagin and grabbed him by the throat. "Just what are you talking about?" he demanded.

"Ask Charley-boy, Bill. Ask Charley. Your Nancy has been talking to a lot of people she shouldn't, Bill. She was mighty angry that you got young Oliver shot and then left him for dead when you took him on your job. Your failed job that is."

Bill gave Fagin's throat a vicious squeeze and then dropped him, coughing and wheezing, to the floor. He strode across the room and bent down so that his nose was inches from Charley Bates's face.

"Is it true?" he hissed. Pale-faced, Charley nodded.

"Then she'll pay!" said Bill.

"Wait, Bill, what are you going to do?" wailed Fagin, realising too late that he had provoked Bill beyond reason.

His face white with fury, Bill Sikes strode from the room without giving Fagin a second glance.

"After him, Charley, and see what he's about!" urged Fagin.

Charley did as he was told and dashed out into the night. He followed Bill Sikes through the alleyways. Bill never once looked round, nor left or right, up or down. He strode on without any thought of anything except what he would do when he got home to Nancy.

Charley loitered in the street and watched Bill push open his door. He heard the heavy creak of the floorboards as Bill climbed the stairs. He heard voices raised in argument for no more than a minute, and then he heard a loud crash.

Moments later, Bill emerged once more onto the street, running now.

As the first grey of dawn began to creep across the sky, Charley crept through the door that Bill had left swinging and climbed the stairs. Nancy lay dead on the floor, bleeding from a wound to the head.

CHAPTER 5

WRONGS ARE RIGHTED

WORD of the murder spread across London fast, and soon both the police and the general public could think of nothing other than catching the monster who had committed the crime.

With nowhere else to hide, Bill returned to Fagin's room, where his sanity seemed to deteriorate by the hour as if he were haunted by what he had done.

It was Charley Bates who gave them up. Witnessing Dodger getting sentenced to be transported to Australia followed up by the sight of Nancy's corpse had broken any bond of loyalty that Charley felt to Fagin and Bill.

When Bill heard the shouts of the police outside, he was up on the roof of the building in a flash. There was a great cry from the street as he was seen leaping from one roof to the next.

A number of police officers entered Fagin's room and arrested the old man and the boys, while several others, roared on by an angry mob, tracked Bill's progress across the rooftops.

Charley was with the mob, and if Nancy's death had horrified him, he was far less concerned when he saw Bill make one leap too many and disappear between two buildings. Bill Sikes gave a short scream as he fell, and it was the last sound he ever made.

48

Nancy and Bill Sikes were both dead, Fagin and the gang of pickpockets were in captivity, and Oliver Twist was finally safe. He sat in a carriage with Rose Maylie, her aunt, Mr Brownlow and a sullen looking young gentleman who never said a word.

Mr Brownlow had announced they were to visit Oliver's hometown to establish a few facts about Oliver's history that he thought the boy might find interesting. Despite all that had befallen him at the workhouse and then at Sowerberry the undertaker's, Oliver was full of nervous excitement and, as he began to recognise the hedges and lanes he had travelled when he fled to London, he struck up a breathless commentary on the landscape.

As they approached the town and then drove through its narrow streets, it was all his fellow passengers could do to prevent Oliver leaping out of the carriage. There was Sowerberry's the undertaker's just as it used to be, only smaller than he remembered it.

There were all the well-known shops and houses. There was the workhouse, with its gloomy windows frowning on the street. There was nearly everything as if he had left it yesterday, and all his recent life had been but a happy dream.

They drove straight to the door of the best hotel in town, and were soon seated around a table inside, as Mr Brownlow called the meeting to order and produced a bundle of papers.

"Oliver," began Mr Brownlow, kindly. "You are about to learn a good deal about your past, about your parents, and about why some of the events of the past few weeks have occurred.

"The first thing that you need to know," Brownlow continued, gesturing at the sullen gentleman from the carriage, "is that this fellow here is your half-brother. The second thing you need to know is that he has schemed and plotted against you for some time. We are here to put a stop to that."

Oliver's mouth hung open. He felt as if his whole life, his whole world, were spinning around this very moment.

"Monks! That is what he has been calling himself. Monks here, is now going to explain everything that he has done in relation to Oliver, and if he does not then he will be handed over to the police. Now Monks, speak!"

With the utmost reluctance, Monks began his story. He told of how his father and mother had separated. He told of how his father had fallen in love again with a beautiful young woman named Agnes, who had become pregnant just before his father's sudden and untimely death. He told of how Agnes had been left with no money, and how she had given birth in the workhouse.

"Is he talking about my mother?" Oliver interrupted, very quietly. Mr Brownlow nodded, and Monks continued.

"I wanted to prevent you from ever finding out who your mother was," he said, not

looking at Oliver. "Because I wanted to keep all of our father's money. He left a will leaving his money to you and your mother but I destroyed it. Then I paid Fagin to get you into trouble with the law, thinking that you would be sent to Australia."

"Your father's will is the first thing we will put right," said Brownlow. "Monks here has signed papers, before witnesses, transferring all of your father's remaining wealth to you, Oliver."

Not for the first time, Oliver was too stunned to speak. Rose squeezed his hand gently.

"How did you find all this out, Mr Brownlow?" she asked.

"By remarkable coincidence, Oliver's father was a very close friend of mine and it so happened that he confided in me before his death. He also gave me a portrait of Agnes, your mother, Oliver, which now hangs in my study. When I saw you next to the portrait it struck me as possible that you might be her child. Your story and your age supported the theory.

"And when Rose and I learned from Nancy, God rest her soul, that there was a young man in London seeking to remove all traces of Oliver's identity, it seemed to me quite likely that the young man might be my friend's son from his failed marriage.

"I tracked him down and mentioned that I had information about you, Oliver, and he came readily enough. Then I presented him with my accusations and offered him a choice: that we involve the police, or that he give up his wrongful claims to his father's money, and confess all to us here."

And that is how the last of Oliver's enemies was defeated. Monks left, never to return. Oliver was able to learn all about his mother and father. And Rose …

… Yes, there is one more thing that must be told before this story is complete. Mrs Maylie made a revelation of her own. Agnes, Oliver's mother, left behind a younger sister when she died, by the name of Rose. Rose was only a few years old at the time, and when her parents then also died, and left her an orphan, she was adopted as a niece by one Mrs Maylie.

On learning that they were, in fact, aunt and nephew, Rose and Oliver wept for joy, and swore they would remain close together as long as they lived. Mr Brownlow adopted Oliver and they moved to live in the same village as the Maylies so that Oliver's youthful years from that time on were so happy as to almost make amends for the years of suffering that came before.

THE END